How to
Cheat
at
Visual Aids
Old Testament

Artwork by Pauline Adams
Text by Judith Merrell

Scripture Union

Scripture Union, 207–209 Queensway, Bletchley, Milton Keynes, MK2 2EB, England.

© Pauline Adams and Judith Merrell 1997

First published 1997

ISBN 1 85999 161 0

British Library Cataloguing-in-Publication Data
A catalogue record for this book is available from the British Library.

Cover design by Ross Advertising & Design Limited.
Cover illustration by Pauline Adams.

Printed and bound in Great Britain by Ebenezer Baylis & Son Limited, The Trinity Press, Worcester.

CONTENTS

Welcome to...
How to cheat at visual aids!

How to cheat at visual aids Old Testament is the sequel to an earlier book that covered key stories in the New Testament – although, since the Old precedes the New perhaps we should call this book a 'prequel'!

The first book included pictures of Jesus and the main events in his life; his miracles and parables; Peter and Paul; the key festivals (Christmas, Palm Sunday, Easter, Pentecost); Bible characters in action (running, walking, sitting, lying, listening); pictures representing jobs and professions; animals, crowds, scenery, buildings and props.

This book covers the main stories in the Old Testament, in particular those that might appeal to children. If you don't find the picture you need here, it's worth having a look in the earlier book which includes several pages of general Bible figures.

Why visual aids?

A leader asked a small girl in her group, 'What are you drawing?'

'I'm drawing a picture of God,' came the reply.

'But no one knows what God looks like,' said the astonished teacher.

'They will when I've finished!' said the girl.

Children just love looking at pictures, but they also need them in order to understand a story. Although we have no idea what God looks like, we can guess how the characters in the Bible might have looked. All the pictures in this book have been produced to help you create illustrations to go with Old Testament stories.

A teacher divided his class in half. He told one half of the group a story with pictures, and the other half the same story without any illustrations at all. As you might guess, the group shown the pictures had a better grasp of the story and remembered the key facts for longer than the other group. The illustrations acted as a memory trigger. The children remembered first the pictures and then the story. The moral is clear: if we are going to take the time to tell a Bible story, it is worth making extra effort and preparing some visual aids too.

Using a photocopier

Now that you have bought this book, you have the right to photocopy all the artwork in it, provided you do not use them in any publication offered for sale. Photocopy the pictures you require, then cut them out and paste them onto a background or plain sheet of paper, to create the scene you need. Next, photocopy the finished picture. If your final photocopy reveals lines where you have cut round the pictures, simply adjust the light/dark button on your photocopier until these disappear. Remember – all the pictures can be enlarged or reduced on a photocopier. This means that you can place large figures in the foreground and smaller figures in the background to create a sense of perspective. Equally, you can reduce a picture to a fraction of its size to provide a tiny illustration in the corner of a service sheet; or enlarge it over and over again to create an A4 or even an A3 flashcard. The possibilities are endless.

The artwork in this book can be photocopied onto acetate for use with an overhead projector. See the first *How to Cheat...* book for further information on using pictures with overhead projectors, flashcards and story figures, plus how to draw simple figures, faces and backgrounds.

Make a
model
theatre

Find a sturdy cardboard box and turn it into a model theatre. The kind of box that contains A4 paper for the photocopier works extremely well. Remove the top of the box and cut out the two sides, leaving a triangle of card at each corner to prevent the sides collapsing. Finally, cut a large window in the front panel.

Draw or copy suitable pictures to attach to the back of the box as background scenery. You might find something suitable on pages 81 to 85. It is also worth looking in the New Testament *How to cheat at visual aids!* If the story has several scenes, have ready a variety of backgrounds that can be fixed in place with *Blu-tack*. You may like to photocopy and enlarge the curtains below, to fix in front of the stage as you change the scene. These can be attached with *Blu-tack* or fixed to a piece of dowel that can be slotted through a hole in each side. The theatrical logo is designed to fix to the front of your model theatre.

Photocopy the characters who appear in your story, and paste each one onto thin card. Attach a narrow strip of card to the base of each figure so that they can be slid in and out of the theatre as the story progresses.

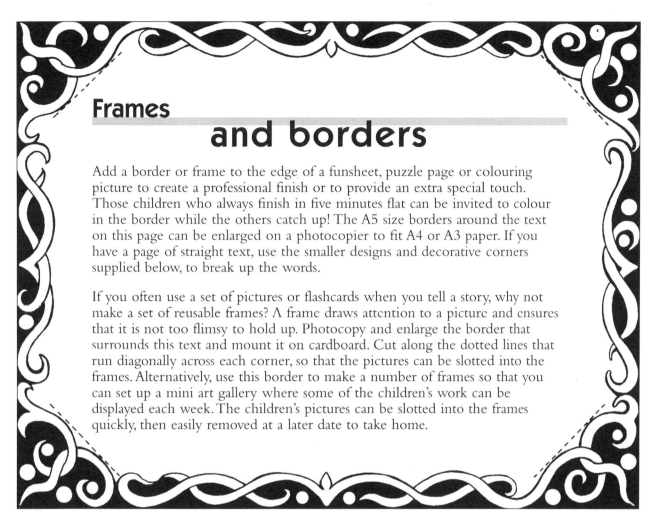

Frames
and borders

Add a border or frame to the edge of a funsheet, puzzle page or colouring picture to create a professional finish or to provide an extra special touch. Those children who always finish in five minutes flat can be invited to colour in the border while the others catch up! The A5 size borders around the text on this page can be enlarged on a photocopier to fit A4 or A3 paper. If you have a page of straight text, use the smaller designs and decorative corners supplied below, to break up the words.

If you often use a set of pictures or flashcards when you tell a story, why not make a set of reusable frames? A frame draws attention to a picture and ensures that it is not too flimsy to hold up. Photocopy and enlarge the border that surrounds this text and mount it on cardboard. Cut along the dotted lines that run diagonally across each corner, so that the pictures can be slotted into the frames. Alternatively, use this border to make a number of frames so that you can set up a mini art gallery where some of the children's work can be displayed each week. The children's pictures can be slotted into the frames quickly, then easily removed at a later date to take home.

Captions and labels

If you display their collages and pictures on the wall for others to appreciate, children will realise how much you value their contribution. Their work can always be taken home at a later date, giving them the opportunity to share a Bible story they have heard with the folk at home. In either case, why not create a caption or label to stick on the children's artwork? A short caption will help others to understand the significance of what they are doing.

The decorative alphabet below can be photocopied and enlarged to provide short captions (eg 'Thank you, God') or perhaps the name of the relevant Bible character (eg Daniel or Elijah). If you enlarge the letters to mount on a display, invite individual children to colour each letter.

When a longer caption is required, you could ask someone with a personal computer to print out the words for you.

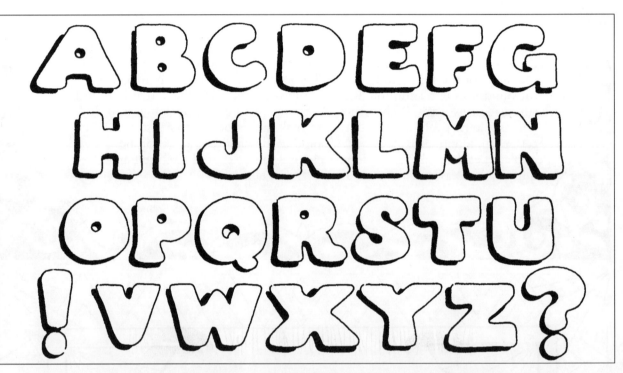

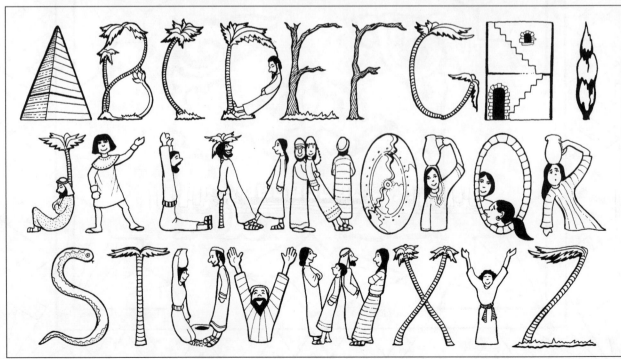

Puzzle pages

The pictures in this book can be used to create worksheets for your holiday club. (Calling them 'funsheets' sounds far more appealing!) Or you could use them to illustrate a children's page for the church magazine. Here are some ideas.

Wordsearches

Wordsearches are always popular with children. Words can be hidden vertically or horizontally inside a grid of letters. If you have older children in your group, try having some of the words go diagonally across the grid, or even backwards. For a mixed age group, you could include a mystery word, to challenge the older ones and to slow them down so that they don't finish too far in advance of everyone else.

Place a wordsearch alongside a relevant picture to colour and you have something to appeal to different tastes, or perhaps to the younger and older children in your group. Sometimes it's fun to base a wordsearch on a picture. Simply mark with a star anything in the picture which has been included in the wordsearch.

To ask a group of children to hunt for ten or twelve words can be a somewhat pointless exercise unless you make the most of the chance to reinforce the Bible story you have just told. It's often a good idea to write a summary of your Bible story and to ask the children to find the words that are underlined. Alternatively, write a number of questions on the Bible story and hide the answers in the grid. In this way the children are revising the story as they work. Our sample wordsearch is based on the story of Moses in the basket. Can you find the mystery word?

To save his **life**, baby **Moses** was hidden in a basket and floated down the river. His sister Miriam watched from her hiding place in the **reeds**. She saw an Egyptian **Princess** discover the **basket** and rescue her **baby** brother. Miriam offered to find someone to help the Princess take care of the baby. She went straight home and fetched her **mother**! **God** had a very special **plan** for Moses, a plan that would save the people of **Israel**.

Wordsearches don't always need to be square, try a tree-shape or a Bible house-shape. Or go one better and design a grid to fit the story – a whale-shaped grid for Jonah, an ark-shaped grid for Noah, and so on!

Spot the difference!

'Spot the difference' pictures are easy to create and popular with younger children. Photocopy your chosen picture twice, then use a fine black pen and a bottle of correction fluid to make a few alterations to the second picture. Invite the children to spot the differences and circle them on the second picture with a felt-tipped pen. Finally, encourage them to colour in the first picture. Can you spot ten differences between these two pictures of Jacob and Joseph?

Complete the picture

Photocopy an illustration that goes with your Bible story, then remove part of the picture. You could cut a Bible character in half straight down the middle and ask the children to draw in the other side. Or you could remove the lower half of the picture and get them to complete the picture from the waist down. Or just leave the head and feet, and let them draw in the costume.

It is often fun to set the scene or give a reason for this exercise. For example, in your instructions, you could explain that the artist ran out of time, inviting the children to help him finish the picture. Or use a bottle of correction fluid to white-out parts of the picture. You could always say you were whitewashing the ceiling and some paint fell on the picture!

Masks

Masks are fun to make and children are always thrilled to take one home at the end of a session. Masks enable children to adopt a completely new identity and to mime or act out a role. Even shy children often find that a mask gives them confidence to try their hand at acting.

Copy these simple outlines onto paper. Or, if you are feeling artistically challenged, enlarge the pictures several times over on a photocopier to achieve the right size. Then photocopy one outline for each child. Your photocopier may be one that takes thin card; if not, let the children colour the pictures and paste them onto card. The back of a cornflakes packet works well. Cut out the eye and mouth holes, and attach a piece of elastic to the sides.

You might like to make the masks with your group just for the pleasure of it, as part of a craft activity. Alternatively, you could use the masks as a way of telling a story through drama or mime.

A leader makes a mask and tells a story in role, or the children make masks and take part in acting out the story.

You could make several lion masks and tell the story of Daniel in the lion's den from the point of view of the hungry lions who mysteriously find that they can't open their mouths! Or use the Egyptian Princess mask to tell the story of baby Moses in the basket. A friendly camel can be an onlooker in almost any Bible story with an outdoor setting. The simplest way to use the masks as part of a sketch is to ask one or two people to narrate the story, while those with masks mime the actions centre stage.

7

8

9

11

12

13

14

15

16

17

18

19

20

21

22

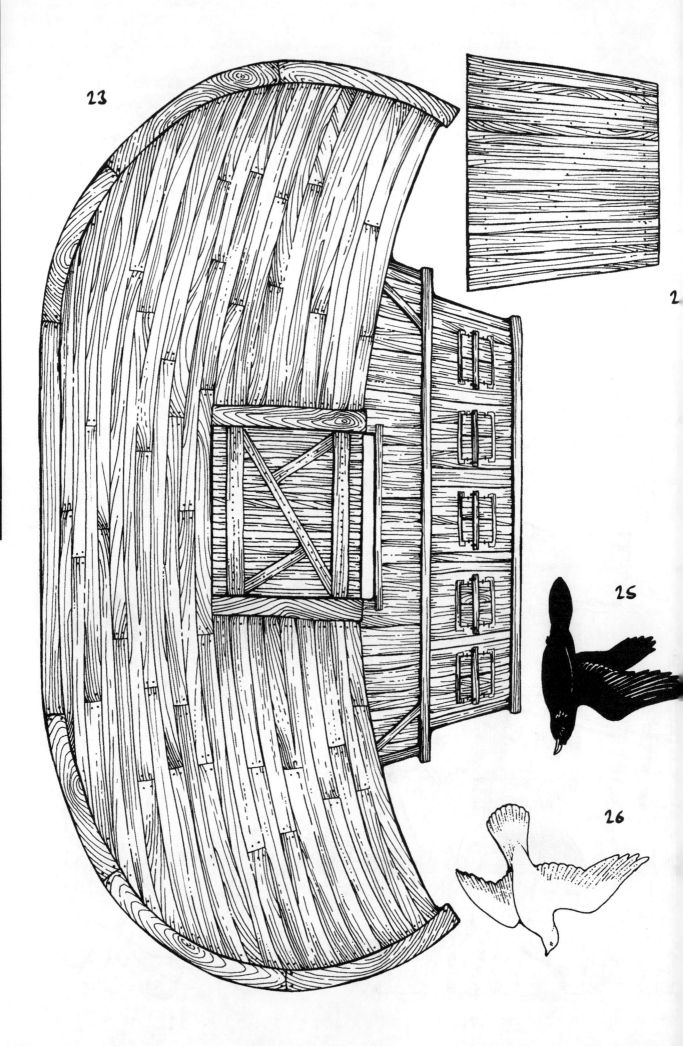

23

24

25

26

7

8

29

31

32

34

35

36

43

45

44

47

48

49

50

51

52

53

S4

S6

S5

S7

S8

S9

60

61

62

63

64

65

66

67

68

69

70

71

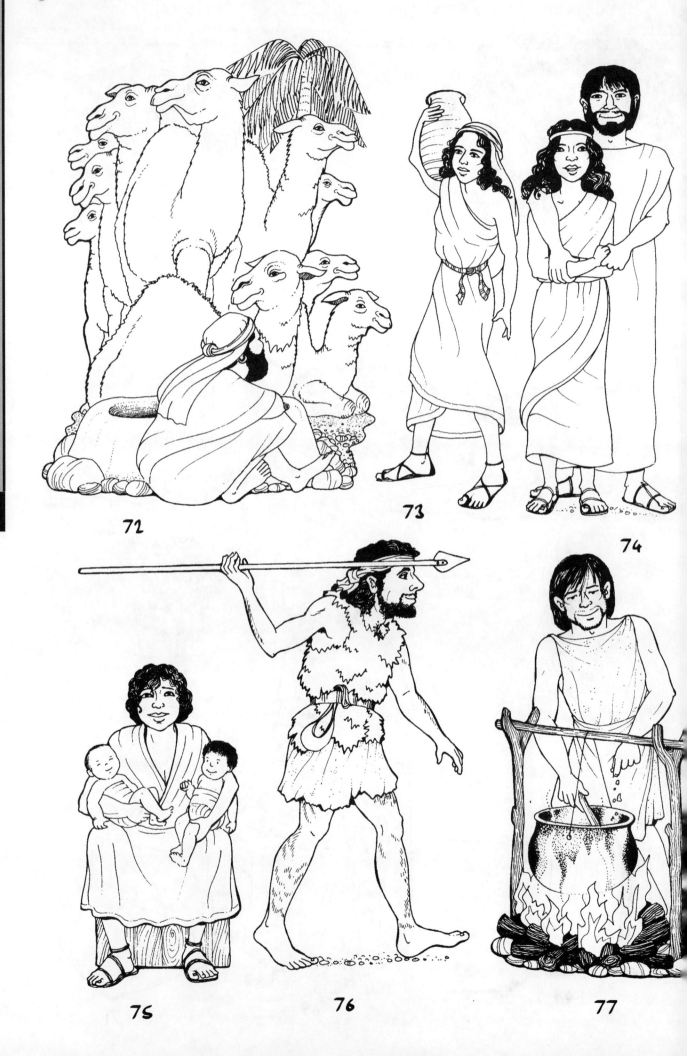

72

73

74

75

76

77

78

79

80

Haran

82

81

83

84

85

86

87

88

89

90

91

92

93

94

95

96

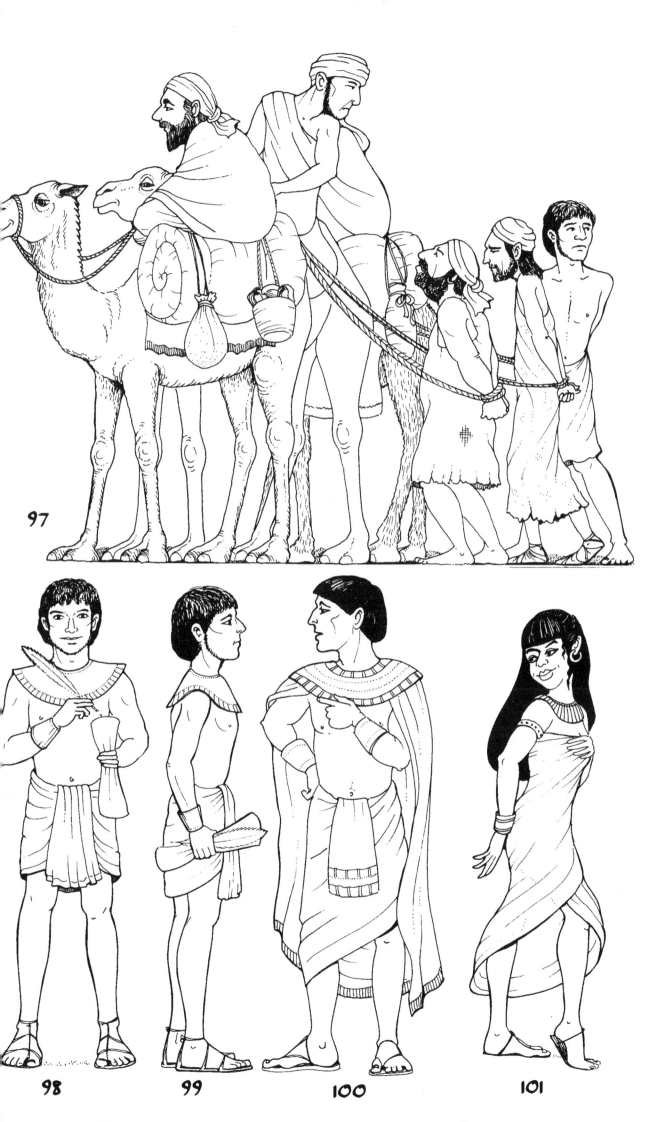

97

98   99   100   101

102

103

105

106

10

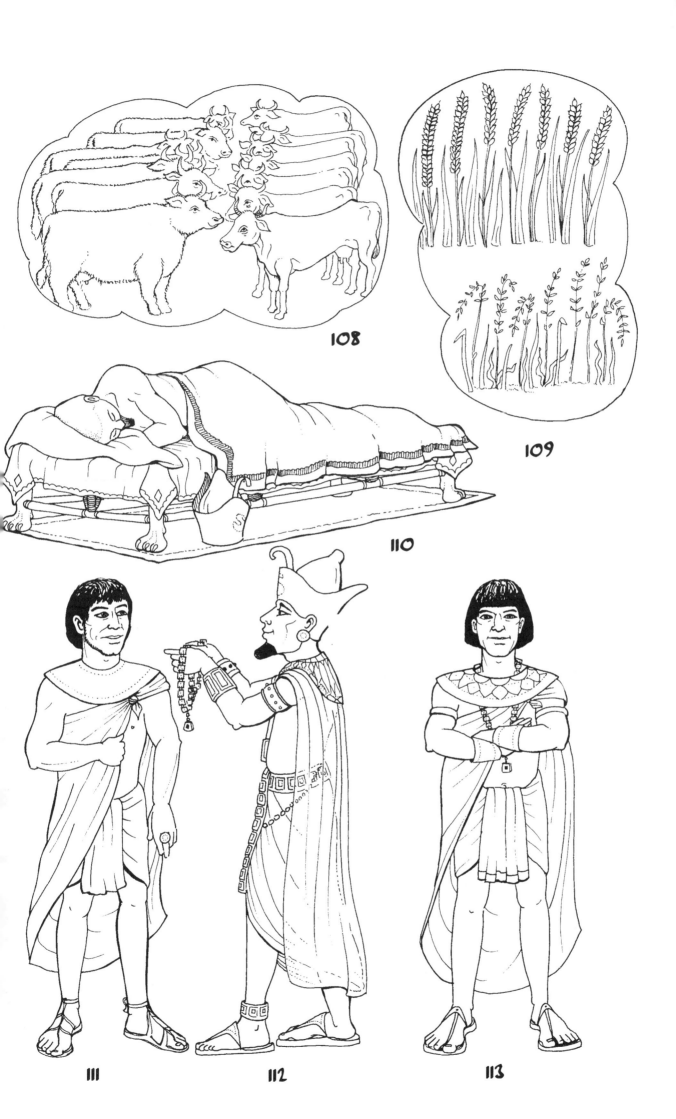

108

109

110

111

112

113

114

115

116

117

118

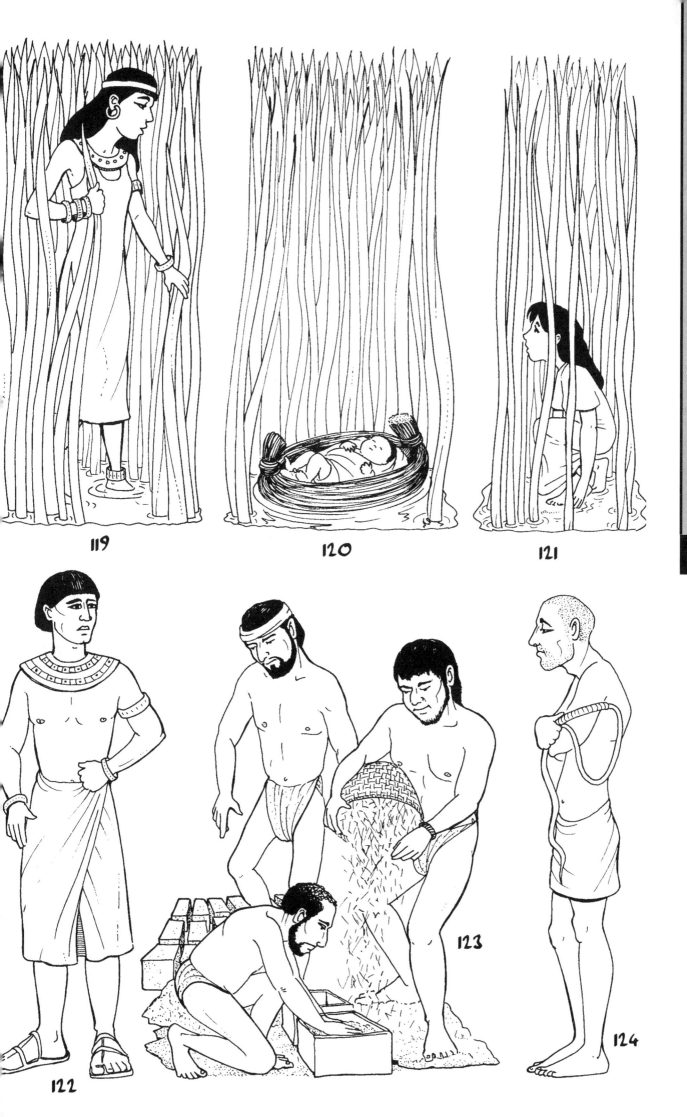

119

120

121

122

123

124

125

126

127

128

129

130

131

132

133

134

135

136

137

138

139

140

141

142

143

145

146

147

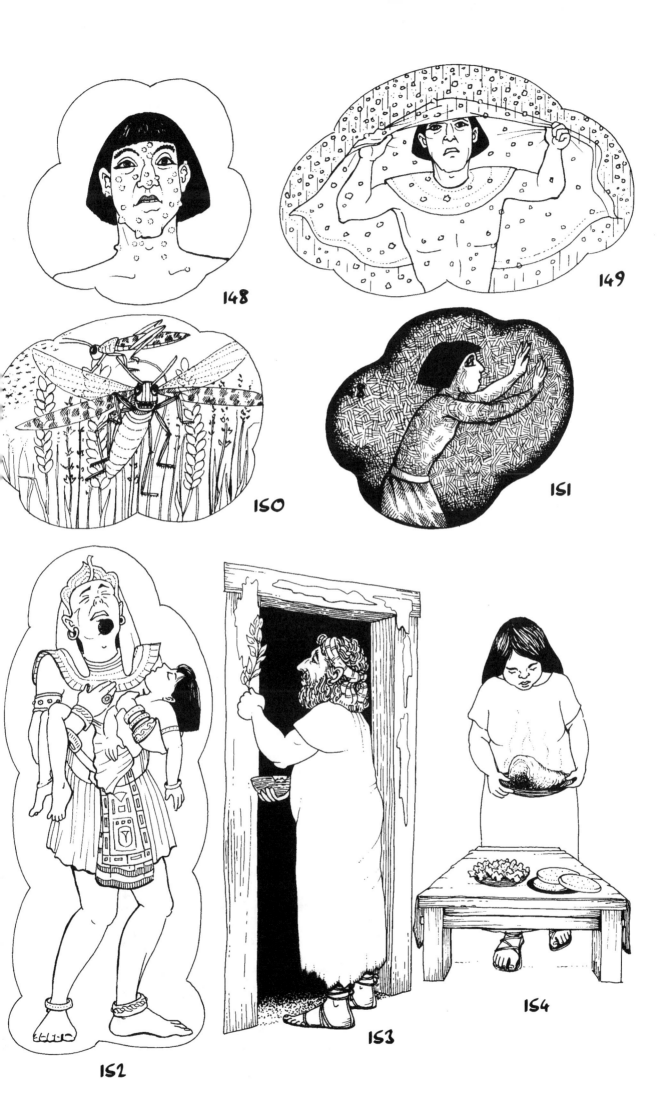

148

149

150

151

152

153

154

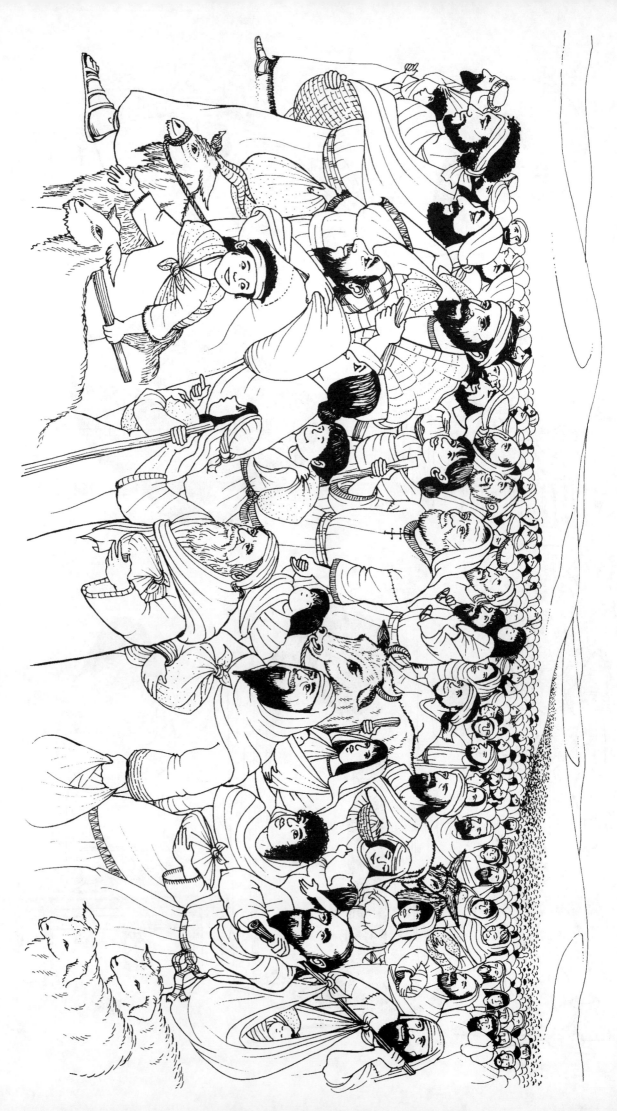

ISS

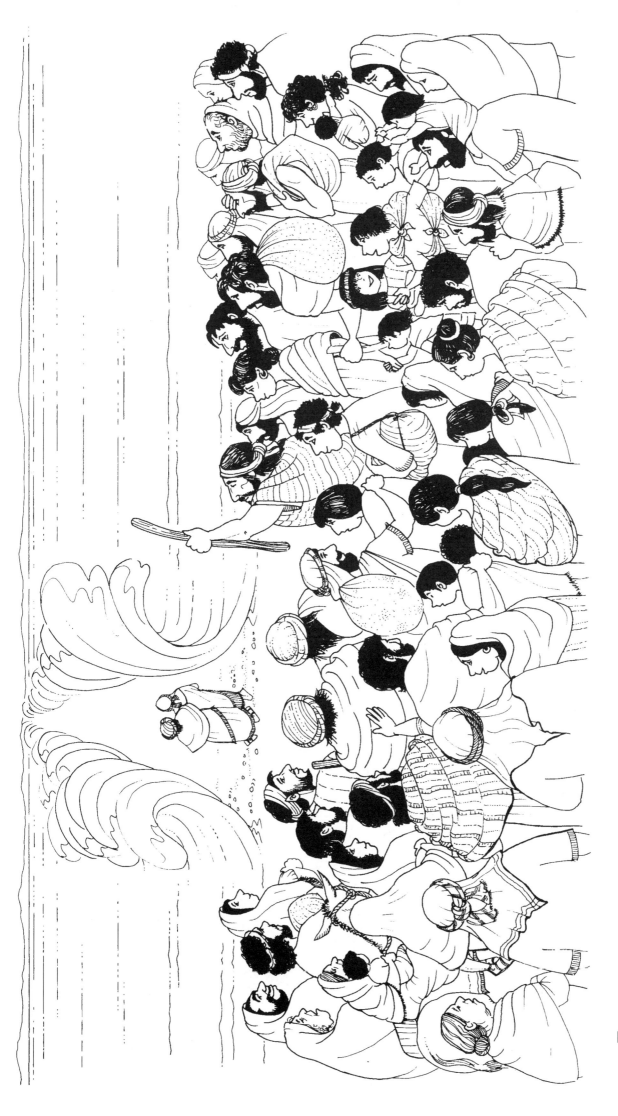

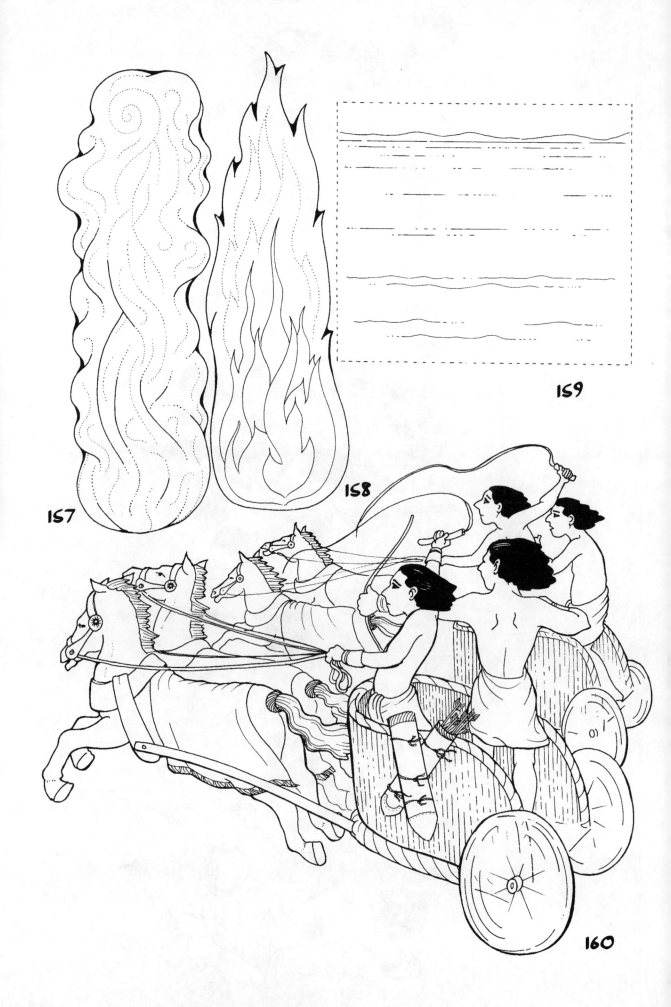

157

158

159

160

161

162

163

164

165

166

167

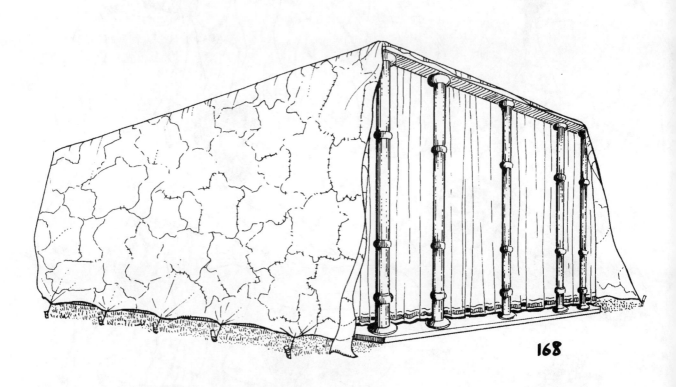

168

169

170

171

172

173

174

175

176

177

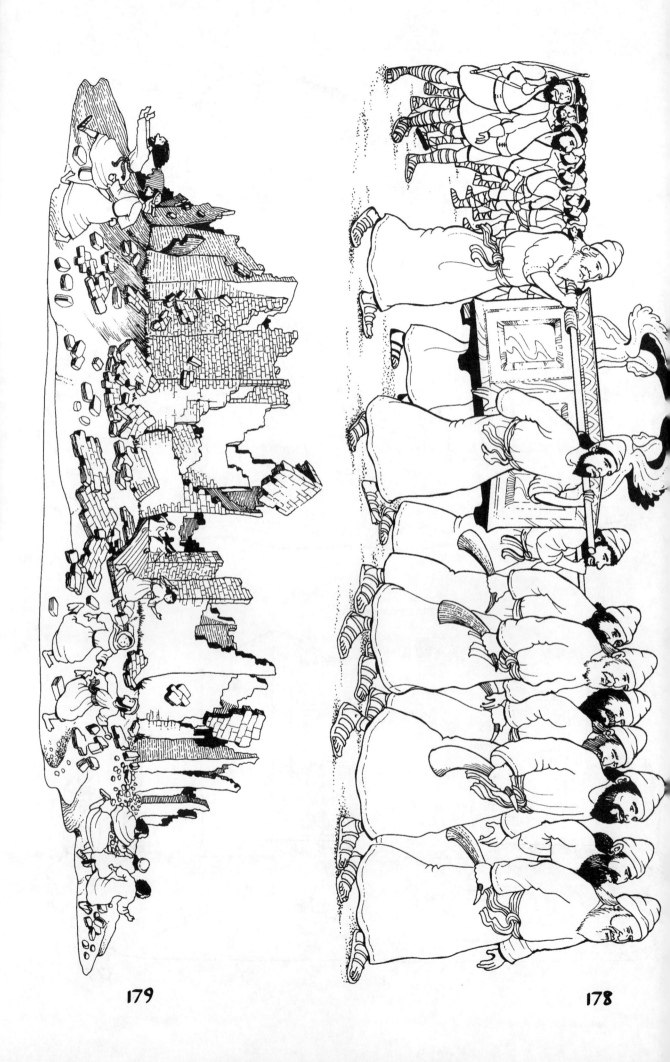

179

178

181

182

183

184

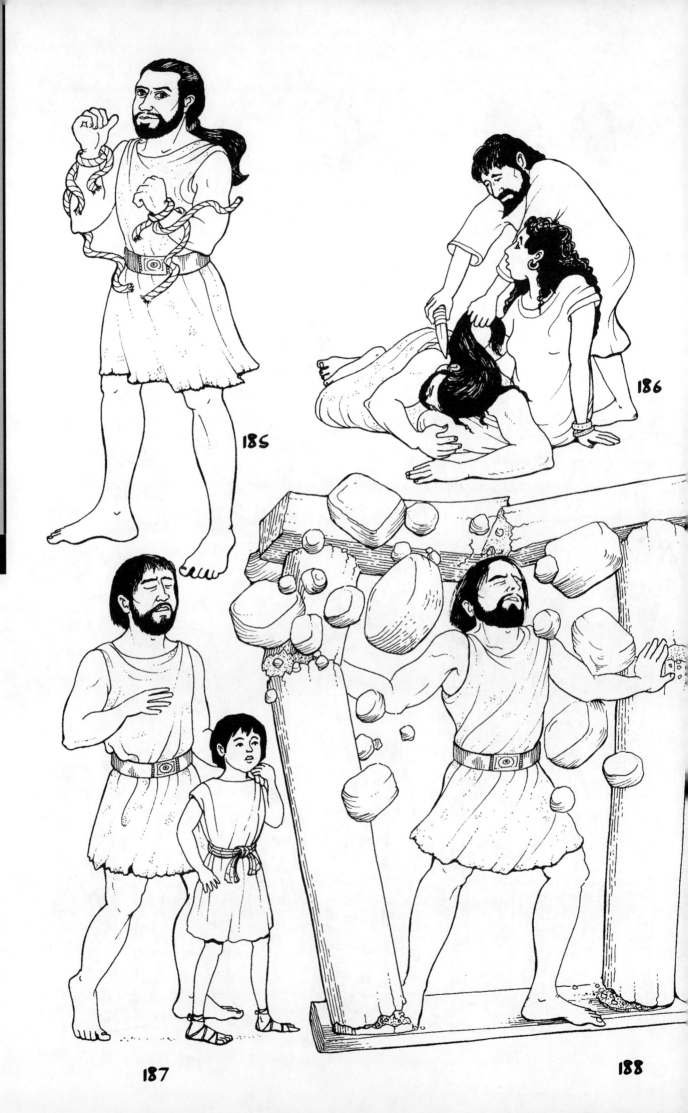

185

186

187

188

189

190

191

192

193

194

195

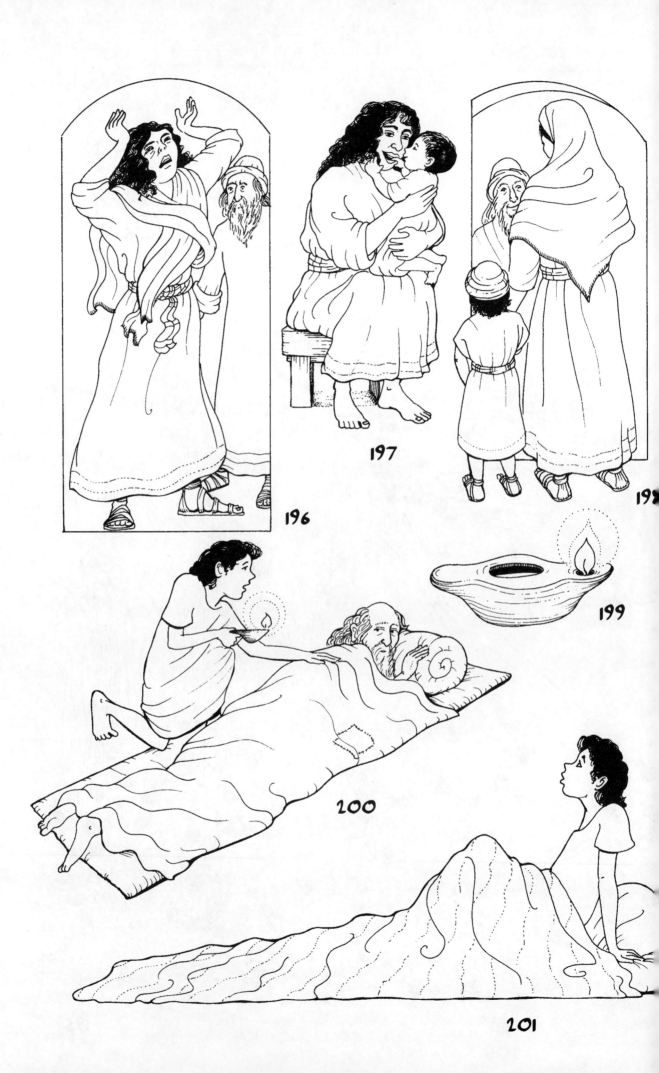

196

197

198

199

200

201

202

203

204

205

206

107

208

209

210

211

212

213

214

215

216

217

218

219

220

222

221

223

224

225

226

227

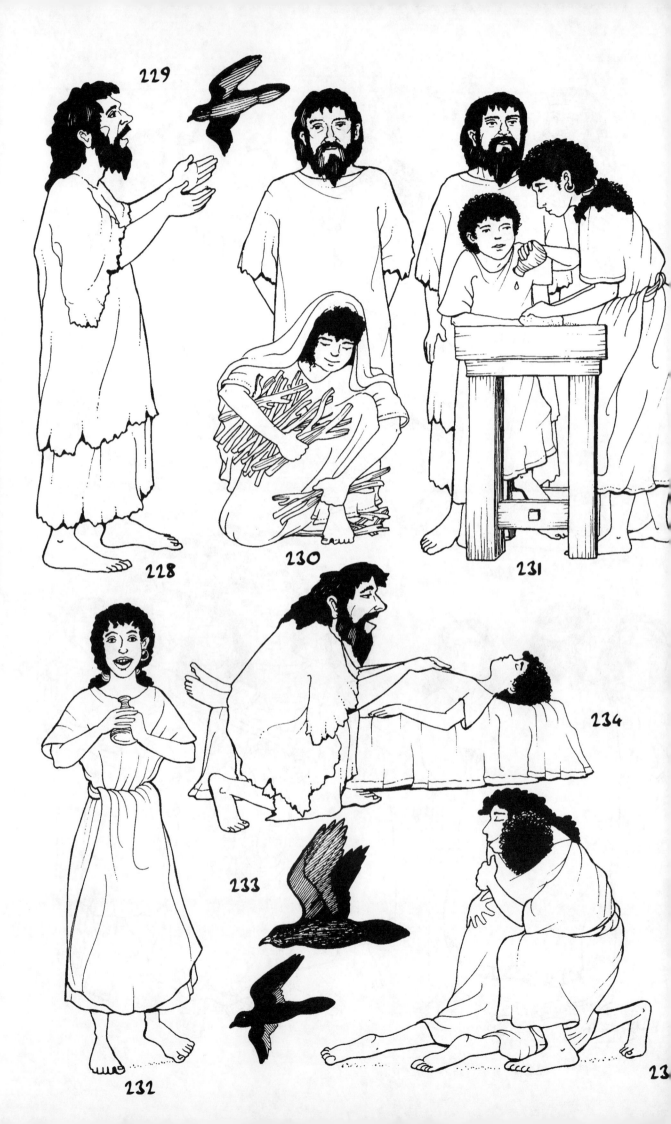

229

228

230

231

232

233

234

23

6

237

238

239

240

241

242

243

244

245

246

247

248

24

250

251

252

253

254

255

256

257

258

259

260

261

262

263

264

265

266

26

268

269

270

271

272

273

274

275

276

278

279

280

281

282

284

285

286

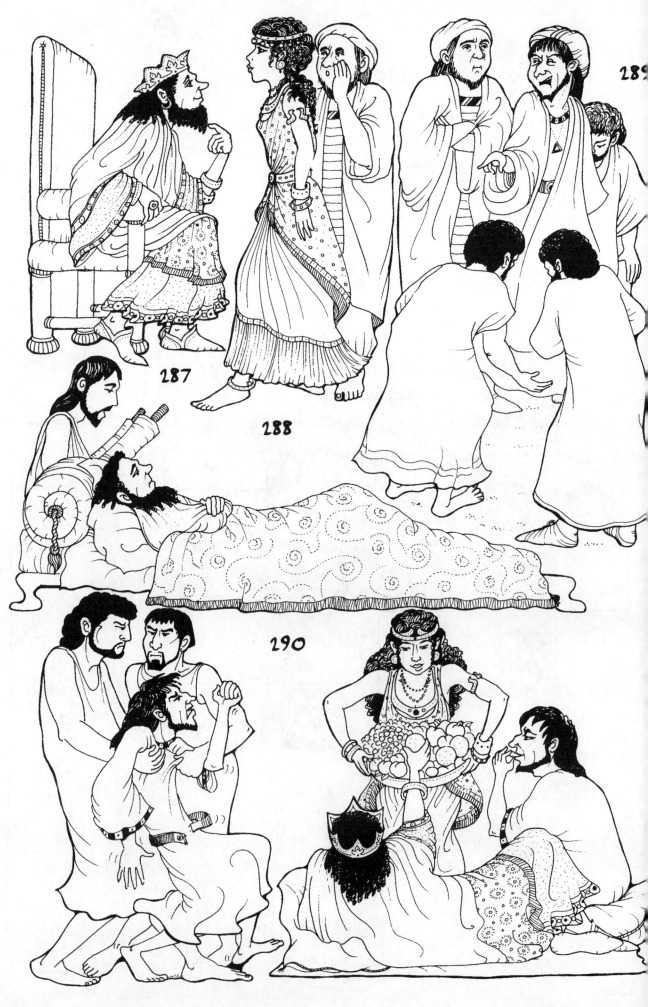

287

288

289

290

291

292

293

294

295

296

297

298

299

300

301

303

304

306

305

307

308

309

310

311

313

314

315

316

mene, mene, tek

317

318

319

320

322

323

325

326

327

328

329

335

336

337

338

339

340

341

342

343

344

345

346

349

347

348

357

352

358

353

356

350

351

354

355

359

360

361

36

36

364

365

366

367

368

369

370

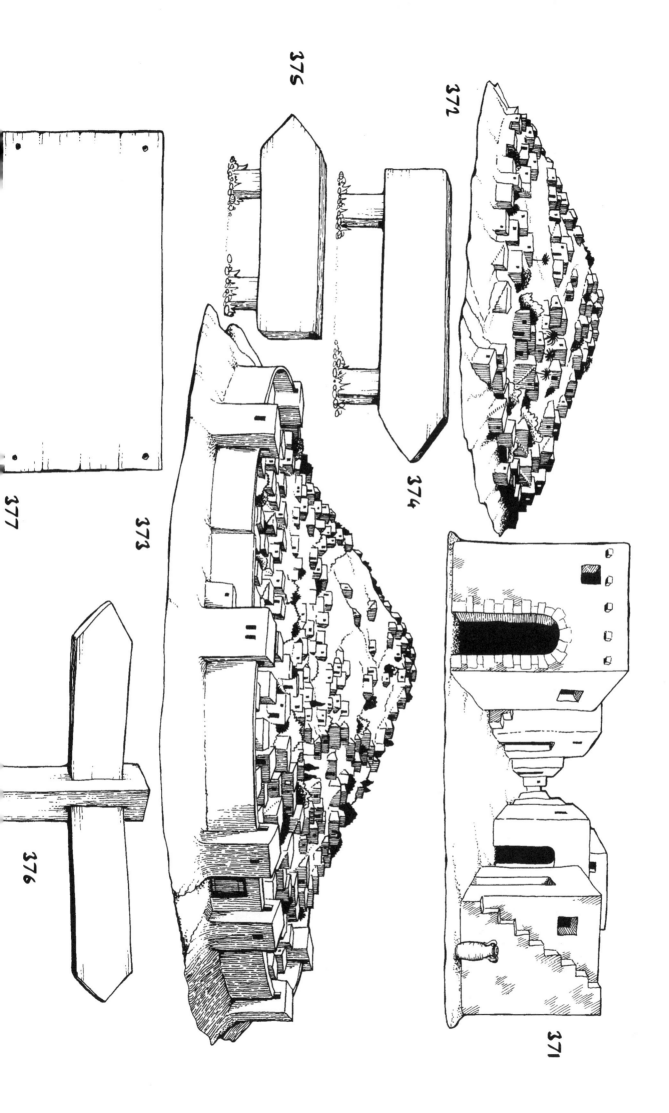

371

372

373

374

375

376

377

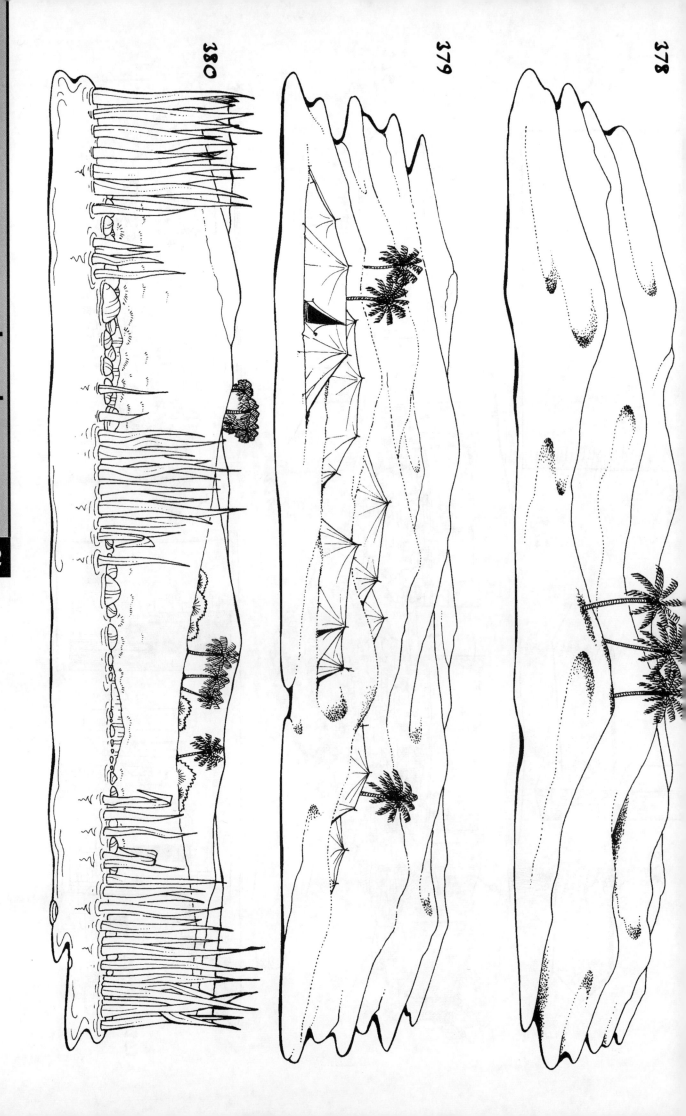

378

379

380

381

382

383

384

385

386

387

388

389

390

391

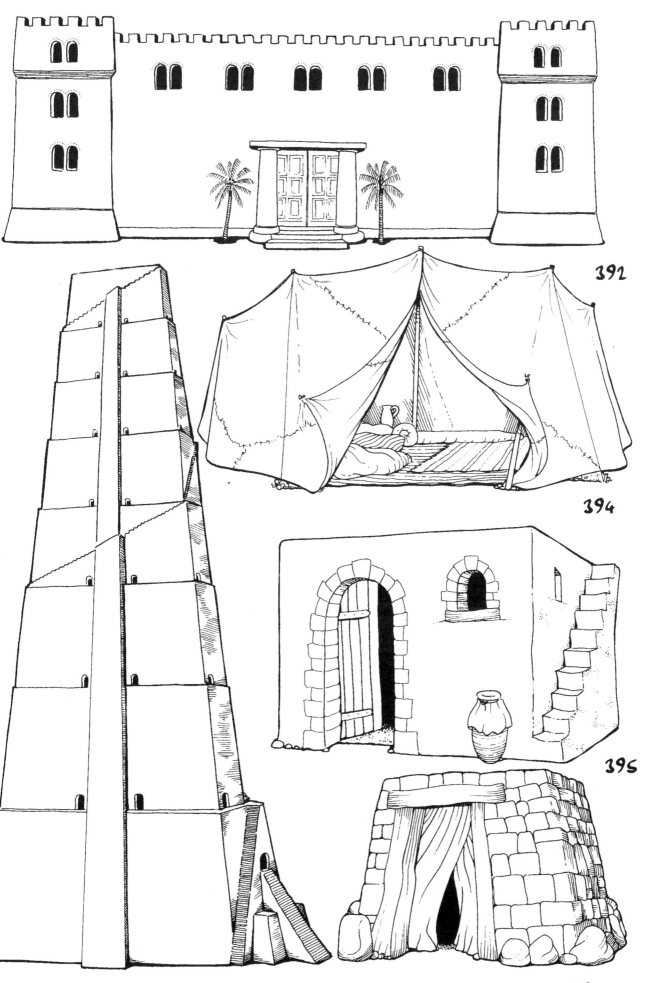

392

394

395

396

3

397

398

399

40

401

402

403

404

405

406

407

408

409

410

411

412

413

414

416

419

417

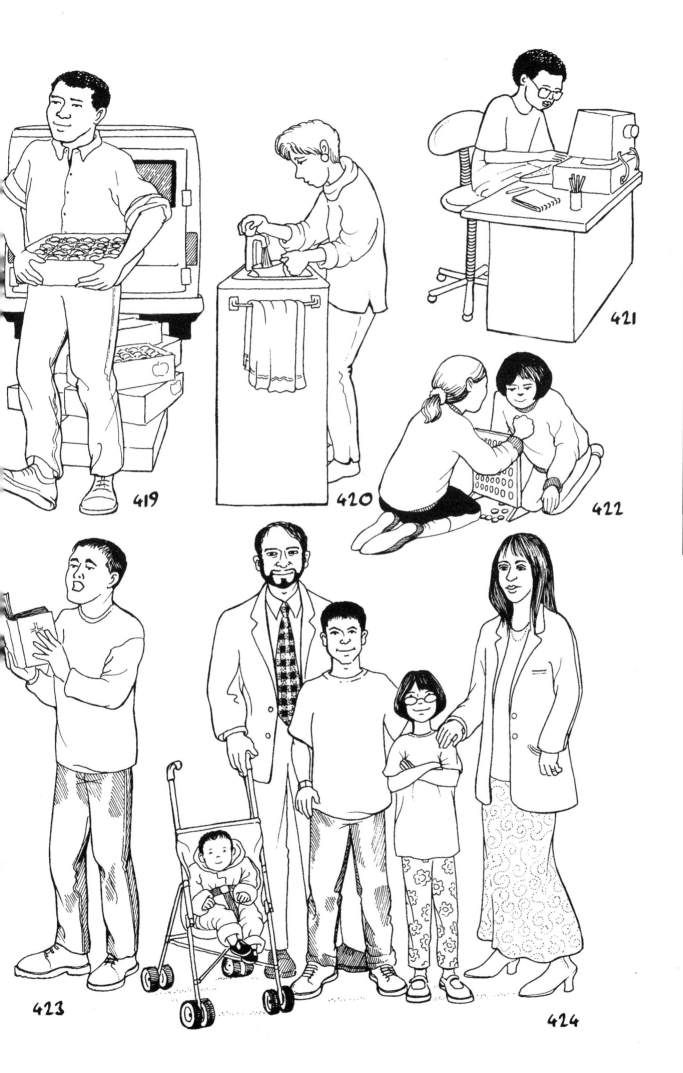

419

420

421

422

423

424

425

426

427

428

429

430

431

432

433

434

435

436

Goliath meets
his match

Narrators 1 and 2 stand stage left and right, reading their lines from clipboards. David and Goliath act their roles centre stage. David and Goliath masks can be found on pp 92–93.

Narrator 1: Ladies—
Narrator 2: And gentlemen!
1: Welcome to the valley of Elah!
2: Welcome to the fight of the century!
1: Let's hear a warm round of applause—
2: For our two contestants.
1: In the left corner—
2: Representing the Philistines—
1: We have Goliath from Gath! *(Enter Goliath who bows)*
2: Goliath the great! *(Goliath flexes his muscles.)*
1: Goliath the giant! *(Goliath stretches.)*
2: He's super fit! *(Goliath jogs on the spot.)*
1: He's fighting fit! *(Goliath punches the air.)*
2: Nearly three metres tall! *(Goliath stands on a chair!)*
1: *(Visibly amazed)* That's … that's nine foot six inches!
2: There's no doubt about it—
1: He's the favourite to win this fight.
2: Now let's meet his opponent – an Israelite!
1: In the right corner we have—
2: Er … we have—
1: In the right corner we have—
2: Er … I don't know. *Who* do we have?
1: In the right corner we have … an Israelite!
2: No, we don't!
1: Yes, we do!
2: No, we don't!
(They go on in similar vein, encouraging the audience to join in).
1: Well, we *should* have!
2: But none of the Israelites wanted to fight.
1: Why not?
2: They were – *(whispers)* scared.
1: *(Shouts)* SCARED?!
2: *(Covers ears)* Yes.
1: The Lord's army? Scared?
2: Yes – and don't shout!
1: Sorry.
Goliath: Cowardy, cowardy custards! Can't fight for mustard!
2: Did you hear that?
Goliath: I challenge any one of you to come and fight me! In fact, I *dare* you to pick someone to fight me!
1: Did you hear that?
2: Goliath went on and on challenging the Israelites—
1: Every morning—
2: And every evening—
1: For forty days.
2: But none of the Israelites took up the challenge.
1: None of them dared.
2: They were far too scared.
Goliath: Scaredy cats! Scaredy cats!
1: And so it went on—
2: Until one day—
1: A young lad called David—
2: Arrived on the scene. *(Enter David.)*
1: David was a shepherd—
2: Young and keen.
1: And he had three older brothers—
2: Who were soldiers in King Saul's army.
1: One day, David's dad said—
2: Right, lad, I want you to go and visit your brothers.
1: I want you to take them ten kilos of grain—
2: And ten loaves of bread—
1: And you'd better take these ten cheeses to the commanding officer—
2: And don't forget to say that Jesse sent them.
David: Yes, Dad! Right away, Dad!
1: Right, lad, off you go. *(David jogs round the outside of the stage.)*
2: When David arrived— *(David returns centre stage, out of breath.)*
1: He left the food with the officer in charge—

2: And went off to find his brothers.
1: He was just in time to hear Goliath issue his challenge.
Goliath: Scaredy cats! Scaredy cats!
David: What's going on? Who's that?
2: 'Ere! It's our little bruvver!
1: Go 'ome, David.
2: Go and look after the baa lambs.
Goliath: Scaredy cats! Scaredy cats!
David: Who's that?
1: That's Goliath.
2: He's the Philistine's prize fighter.
1: If anyone kills him—
2: They'll get a huge reward—
1: Loadsa' money—
2: And the hand of the King's daughter in marriage—
1: And all the Philistine army will become our slaves.
2: But if he fails—
1: We'll lose everything—
2: And we'll become *their* slaves.
1: Now go 'ome, you cheeky brat!
2: And stop asking stupid questions!
David: *I'll* fight him. *I'm* not scared. God will help me. I've killed lions and bears…
1: Ha ha ha!
2: Go 'ome, little boy!
1: But David went and told King Saul—
2: That he was willing to fight.
David: The Lord has saved me from a lion and a bear. So I'll fight this man since none of you dare.
1: So the King lent David his armour—
2: And his sword.
David: Thanks!
(The narrators mime fastening armour onto David, who tries to walk but soon falls over.)
David: This is no good. It's far too heavy.
1: So he gave back the armour—
2: And he took out his catapult.
1: He chose five smooth stones from the stream.
(David bends and mimes choosing the stones.)
2: Then he went out to meet Goliath.
David: Oi! Big guy! I'll fight you!
Goliath: *(Looks all around but doesn't see David.)* What? Did someone say something?
David: *(Shouts and pulls Goliath's sleeve.)* I said, I'll fight you!
Goliath: *(Laughs)* Did you say something, shrimp?
David: *(Shouts louder)* I said, *I'll* fight you!
Goliath: You cheeky brat! Who do you think you are? I'll feed your body to the birds and the wild animals!
David: I'm David, and God is on *my* side. I'm going to cut off your head and feed your body to the birds and wild animals!
Goliath: Ho ho ho! We'll see about that!
1: Ding ding!
2: Round one.
1: *(In dramatic tones)* So Goliath started walking towards David—
2: And David started running towards Goliath.
1: David put a stone in his catapult—
2: He whirled it above his head—
1: Let go—
2: And—
1 & 2: THWACK!
1: The stone hit Goliath smack in the middle of the forehead.
1 & 2: Right there. *(Both point to the centre of their forehead.)*
1: Goliath fell flat on his face—
2: With a broken skull.
1: David took Goliath's sword—
2: And cut off his head—
1: When David held up the giant's head —
2: The Philistines knew that their hero was dead.
1: So they ran away as fast as they could—
2: With the Israelites following in hot pursuit.
(They both pause.)
1: The battle was over, the day was won—
2: And David thanked God for all that he'd done.

Grumpy Jonah

This story can be used with pictures on pp 73–75.

Part 1

(Picture 325)
Jonah gritted his teeth and grumbled. The Lord God wanted him to take a special message to the Ninevites, but Jonah didn't want to go.

'But, Lord,' he complained, 'The Ninevites are dreadful. They're wicked, they're deceitful, they're … a bunch of complete Ninnies!'

But no matter how much Jonah protested, God insisted that he wanted Jonah to go and visit the Ninevites.

(Picture 326)
Then Jonah had a good idea – at least *he* thought it was a good idea. He decided to run away to a far-away country where God would never find him. He hurried down to the harbour in Joppa and climbed on board a ship sailing for Spain.

(Picture 327)
Once on board, he was so exhausted that he curled up below deck and fell fast asleep.

(Picture 328)
The ship sailed into a terrible storm, which left everyone feeling very frightened and sea-sick. The worried sailors woke Jonah up and told him to pray to his God for help. But Jonah knew that the storm was down to him.

'Oh dear,' he told them, 'this is all my fault, because I'm trying to run away from God. Throw me overboard and the storm will die down.'

'We can't do *that*!' said the sailors. But the storm got worse and they soon changed their minds!

(Picture 329)
'We don't normally throw passengers overboard,' said one of the sailors, 'but we're so desperate, we'll try anything!

So, on a count of three, Jonah was dropped into the water with an enormous splash. In an instant the storm died down, and the sailors realised that Jonah's God was a God worth serving.

(Picture 330)
The water was icy cold as Jonah swam around, struggling to stay afloat. Before long, his strength ran out and he felt himself sinking below the waves. Jonah was certain he was going to die, but he was wrong because God had a special plan for him.

(Picture 333–4 placed over no. 330)
He sent a huge fish to swallow Jonah up! It was an *enormous* fish. It may even have been a whale.

(Picture 331)
Jonah lay inside the stomach of the fish for three whole days and nights. It was dark and damp and very, very smelly, just as you might imagine – so

Jonah prayed very, very hard.

The poor fish felt very poorly. He probably wished that he hadn't swallowed Jonah who was rather indigestible! He swam towards the shore and was promptly very sick on the beach.

(Picture 332)
Jonah felt very bedraggled. 'No one will ever believe where I've been the last few days,' he thought to himself.

'Now,' said God, 'Off you go to Nineveh.'
'Oh no!' grumbled Jonah.

(Picture 335)
But this time he did as he was told. He had finally realised that you can't run away from the God who had created the land and sea.

Part 2
Nineveh was an enormous city. It took three days to walk from one side to the other.

(Picture 336)
Jonah had to shout loudly to be heard above the noise of the crowds.

'In forty days Nineveh will be destroyed,' he proclaimed. All the people who heard him realised that they had done wrong.

(Picture 337)
So they took off their fine clothes and wore sackcloth to show how sorry they were. They didn't eat or drink anything for the whole forty days.

'Huh!' thought Jonah to himself. 'These people deserve to die, but I bet God will let them off now. That's the trouble with God – he's far too forgiving!'

(Picture 338)
Jonah sat in the shade of a tall plant and waited to see what would happen. Sure enough, when God saw that the Ninevites had changed their ways, he forgave them and decided not to destroy the city.

'Just as I thought!' grumbled Jonah. So God decided to teach Jonah a valuable lesson.

(Picture 339)
He sent a worm to attack the plant. It withered and died, leaving Jonah to be scorched by the baking sun. Jonah was very angry. 'It just isn't fair! I wish I was dead,' he mumbled.

(Picture 340)
'Jonah,' said God sadly. 'You didn't create that plant, you didn't even water it – yet you feel sorry for it. So why shouldn't I feel pity for the Ninevites. I lovingly created them just as I lovingly created you. That's why I'm ready to forgive them.'

Jonah thought about God's words for a long time. Then he went away and wrote down his story, because he wanted everyone to know just how much God loves them.

Index

Numbers refer to illustrations, except page numbers which are underlined.